MORE SILVER THAN GOLD

FINISHING LINE PRESS
GEORGETOWN, KENTUCKY

ACKNOWLEDGMENTS

Many thanks to our editors and collaborators: Ryan Funk, Junior Clemons,
Claire Chafee, and Jenny Sarris; and to the journals in which some of these poems
and drawings previously appeared, sometimes in different forms: *Transmission,
Eleven Eleven, The Juvenilia,* and *KSAT #9.* "Goreme," "July 18-24," and "July
8-11" were originally published in *It Hasn't Stopped Being California Here.*

Publisher: **Leah Maines**

Editor: **Christen Kincaid**

Cover Design: **Ryan Funk**

Printed in the USA on acid-free paper.
Order online: www.finishinglinepress.com
also available on amazon.com

Author inquiries and mail orders:
Finishing Line Press
P. O. Box 1626
Georgetown, Kentucky 40324
U. S. A.

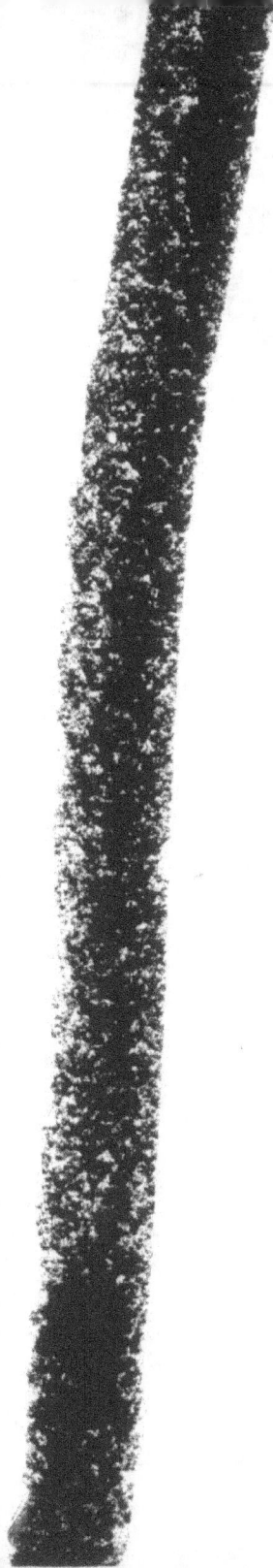

500 CHEMIN DE LA BLAQUE

The cicadas

stopped all at once. Tough

to tell when sound

shifts is or

becomes

      silence. It was

late.

MOAB

The rocks are so red. I asked them what they knew: sea grass. I lied
about energy in the desert to a woman in the desert, I still don't know.
Salt made the rocks soft. She said discipline within pleasure, but
my skin only wants, my habits: gradient. My hips in the red sand.
How could I sleep? When there was water, this was bottom. It's only
something, being human. I asked the canyons since when did living
have to be about the body.

JULY 8-11

Saw some things in Paris made
a list of three but it kept
on: *how*

> *the metro driver turned*
> *his chin girl*
> *in window*
> *checked her pits man kissing woman*
> *hands on her head a pony tail*
> *red elevator*
> *in the middle of the eiffel tower boy hid*
> *his bottle in the bush*

In the haunted house at the carnival a man touched my shoulders
fingers in my hair maybe 30 seconds I yelled *arrêtte ça suffit* it
was the last room all dark my sole cart he howled. After the ride I
grinned hair alive at the roots.

VITRY-SUR-SEINE

Mornings the birds
are dead in twos or six always

chomped through the plume
where it swelled at the breast, white

less blood than I'd imagine
none on the wings just a circle and maggots

organs, but whose teeth
and how quick, or how first?

When I cross the street
consider my body against some

windshield, pass a dog imagine
his bite. I do believe I can out walk anyone

in this city black-eyed men in threes
and fours lean against Deux-cent Cinqs, silver—

are you more lonely than me?
I am loyal, palm to wrist.

The river a compass without
a coast. Ryan writes not to tread lightly

I've decided to always
be sympathetic to anyone chasing

a bus or standing on the curb
necks just so.

BOULDER

Mama
I walked the grid for hours
I'm watching myself talk and talk I'm nervous
this is who I am now without.
I want to have the power
and the control the girls and the people to want me
street after street almost
the middle of the country.
I am making bad decisions
mama, or I'm still all soft
it's hard to say no it's hot in the kitchen
on the carpet it's green I am alone
until I'm not I'm interested in pleasure.

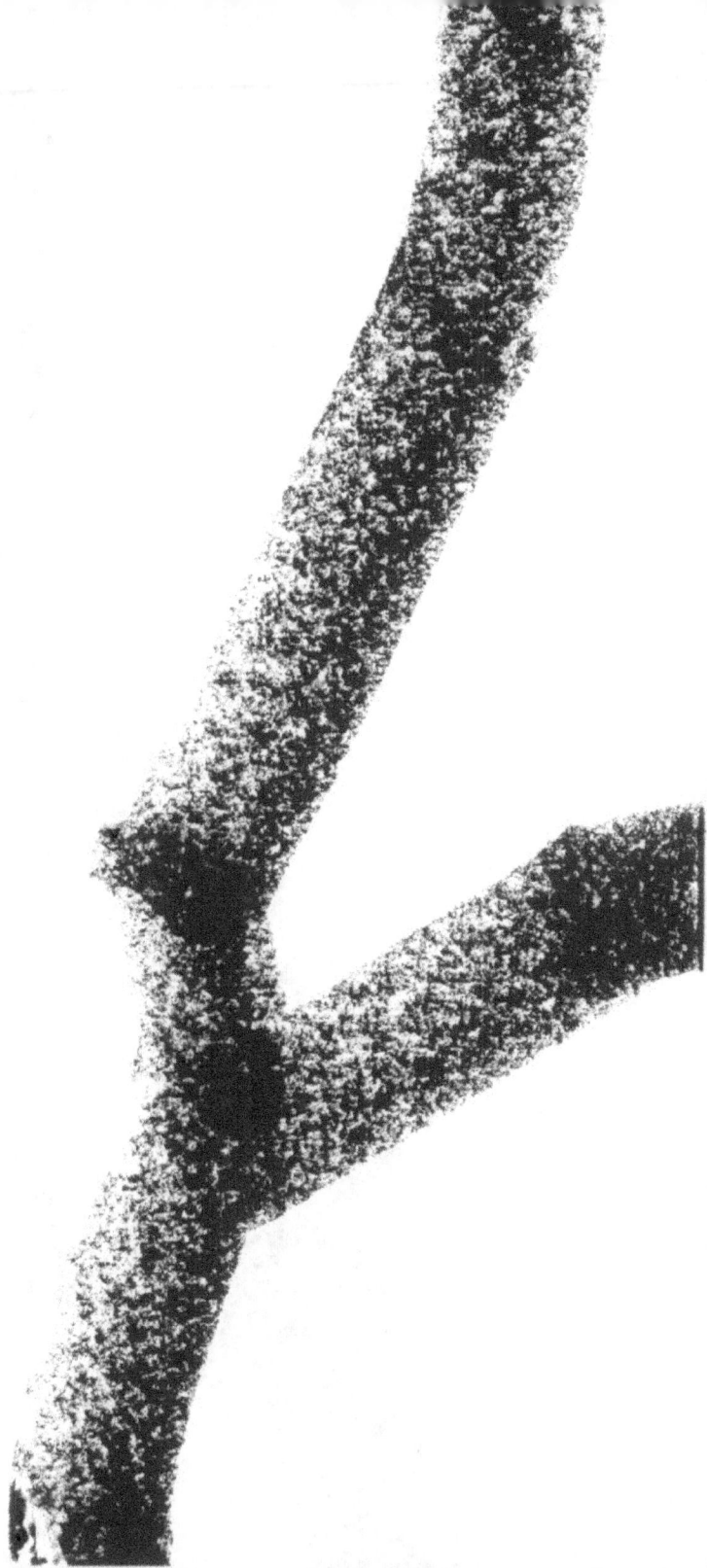

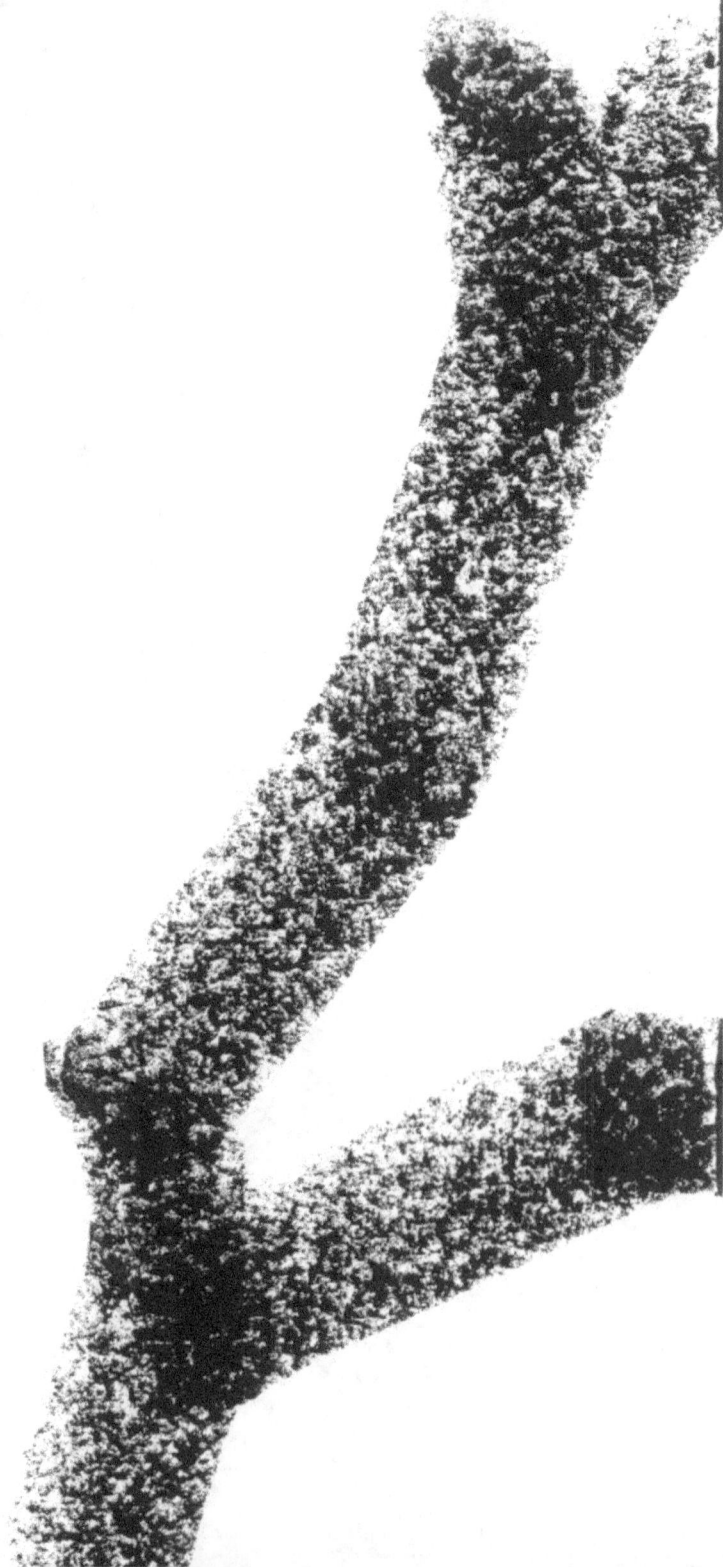

2nd ARRONDISSEMENT

In the hearts of men brick
by brick these banks smell
like piss. We picnic
here pass the bottle bread
again but my body
a shame if not for them.

Nobody cares
about filth so long
as the light
is nice and this city
was built for it.

DIRSEK

To release
desire is what I wanted
most, but how. Asked the sea,
she answered horizon,
cambered. Forever
is an arrow's shot
away. Asked again.
Salt. This I could
understand. The heart
is a muscle. Night after
night I slept like light
on the surface. Moon
said tide.

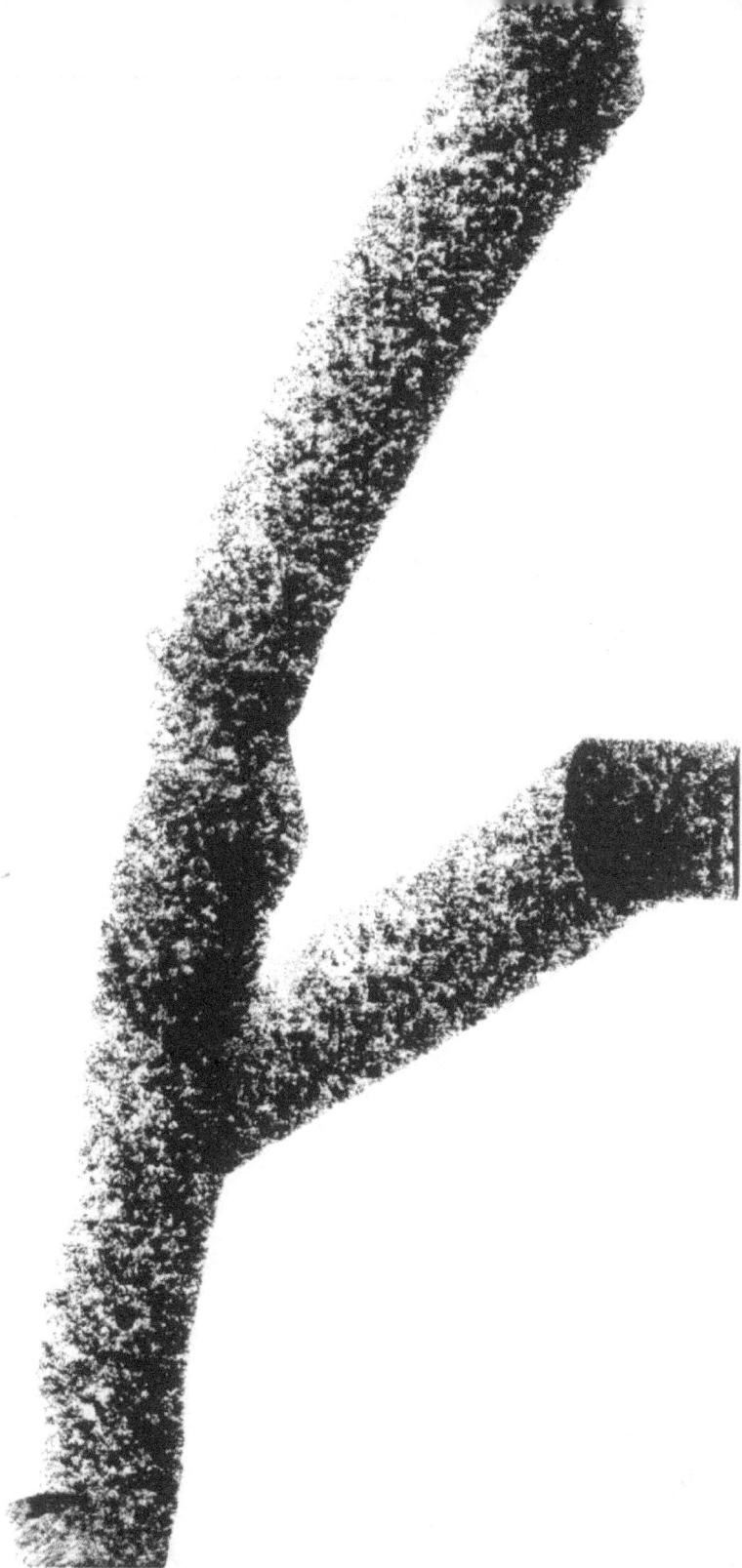

18th ARRONDISSEMENT

We walked for mangos the sun low moving on everything. I said
something because what a duty but then it changed. Men in robes in
street clothes selling DVDs fruit headphones glasses nana tresses *tiens
tiens* a woman bought eye drops. She pedals over stones I lift my feet
knees the whole thing this city a vein never know until where. Then
seine sky again light and how it fell on spires otherwise I've been feeling
like an ant inside.

JULY 18-24

At the table in the evenings I don't speak
because I want to be understood. Learning
my nature through watching others.

When I missed the train I said *merde* but
when the wind spilled my coffee I said fuck.

HOMETOWN

I said I loved a girl,
it was the first time.
Even at night
when it was so pale
I was exactly the same.
I didn't know or was
afraid. Mama,
let sound change
the word.

We drove through rock
I asked how I answered
dynamite.

DOG DAYS

Afraid of my body explained soft spots
to Alice old wood your foot just steps through
like my apartment she said
love. Scratched her shoulder
drank coffee. When
I wake touch my legs thighs so I can
do it again this city I walk
it a luxury
to have nothing but time who's to say
I can't soften the edges of these
days my joints
the room stinks by eleven I'm up.

500 CHEMIN DE LA BLAQUE

Dreamed that she

would come I believed it

for a moment

remembered my crystal

under the pillow meanwhile

cicadas

electric I couldn't

say when.

AVANOS

In the taxi she sings the driver nods
knows it well. It's early we leave the rocks
are pink.

    I drank the milk, I burnt my tongue, I adore you.

ARAPAHOE

Landscapes
are piling up my ribs have never
been so thick. I am
forgetting the words I just
said spoke in Utah
all the girls with eyes
in windows I want
to kiss. For being so
good. The taxi driver
in Denver told me trivia, stuttered
to Elvis, was racist. I'm sleeping
under ceiling fans forgot
what it's like to lie
without a sheet
be so warm.

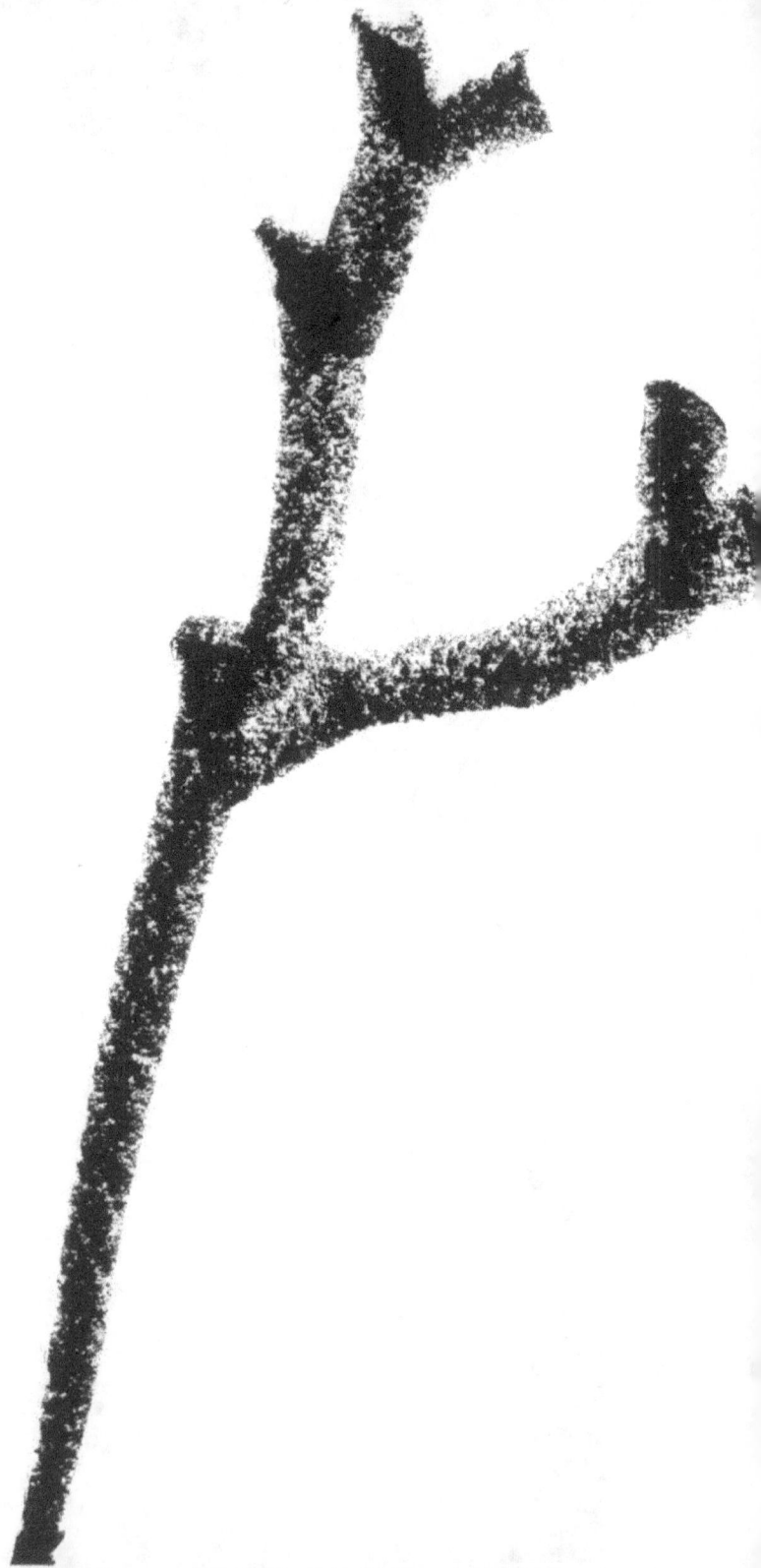

LUYNES

Cicadas at night
nine noon
sun between
shutters still
the days sound
reluctant as if
I was anxious for anything
but presence.

Hold the crystal
with my left hand.

      Birds take turns,
enough sky for all they've got to say.
The morning, my mouth
      all marbles.

GOREME

In that red desert, we expected visions, saw shapes. I slept in my underwear, pollen fell like snow. In this white desert, I want to learn something from shadows. Cigarette butts, sleep. In Pigeon Valley a man shook his tree, cut a walnut from green fruit flesh. Never ate such a pale bitter thing. In Paris, Yasmine found my crystal in a pair of shorts. In Bakersfield, my mom doesn't have air conditioning in her classroom. No matter how I scrub, my skin is dying from the sea.

TO BURLINGTON

You've given me
a kind of message: feathers,
silence. Kissed you
on the solstice, a crystal
in your pocket and me
a stone. Maybe it's time.
Listen to other parts
of my body. The birds
killed daily by this city
give purpose to shovels,
worms.

NEW YORK, SEPTEMBER

Shame, different shapes
and again. I've got reasons.
What is my ambition and why
did the G train scare me so bad.
Then all of a sudden it was fall
had an earache needed socks.
Saw the moon from downstairs
a beige tile tunnel everyone stacked and buried
underneath and cross the street.
   Dear Girl, I tried I know
   I am the bird and I am the rat.
Saw the sunrise over LaGuardia
it was more silver than gold.

PARK SLOPE

About all the fish and food
I've been eating in big European cities

two-horse villages 15-minute suburbs
I write but do not send. In bed

this morning a mosquito
in my ear and it's raining. The birds

in Paris always eaten through always
thought it was me who was eating

you. Been killing
flies all summer every

apartment bus train either I'm awful
good, my palms

or they're just fat and slow.
In another postcard I would

have said you looked beautiful
and more but I haven't decided

what kind of lover to be
besides the kind that waits.

www.ingramcontent.com/pod-product-compliance
Lightning Source LLC
LaVergne TN
LVHW051609080426
835510LV00020B/3198